WRITING WITH MERCURY

For Mike, with love

*and in memory of my parents,
Anne and Einar Mattson*

WRITING WITH MERCURY

Nancy Mattson

*For Roger, Sally
Eluned & Rhianedd
Much love,
Nancy
7/09/06*

Acknowledgements

My thanks to the editors of the following publications in which some of these poems have appeared, sometimes in earlier versions: *Capilano Review, CV2, Northward Journal, Other Voices, PRISM international* and *Secrets from the Orange Couch* (Canada); *THE SHOp* (Ireland); *Manifold, Orbis, Other Poetry, Seam, Staple, The Interpreter's House* and *The Journal* (UK); and the anthologies *My Mother Threw Knives: Poems about Women's Lives* (London: Second Light Publications, 2006); *In Fine Form: The Canadian Book of Form Poetry* (Vancouver: Polestar, 2005); *In the Company of Poets: An anthology celebrating 21 years of readings at Torriano Meeting House* (London: Hearing Eye, 2003); *Juuret Suomessa: Ulkosuomalaisten Runoantologia* (Helsinki: Otava, 1991); *Spiral Bound: An anthology of poetry and songs of genes and their engineering* (London: Hearing Eye, 2000).

'Third Generation Lost Language Blues' was commended in the 1990 League of Canadian Poets National Poetry Contest and published in *More Garden Varieties Two: An Anthology of Poetry* (Toronto: Mercury, 1990).

'"Tosi" is a Word for Truth' was commended and published in the *6th Ware Poetry Competition Anthology* (Ware: Rockingham, 2004).

'When in Finland' won second prize in the Bedford Open Poetry Competition 2002.

I am grateful to all who have helped shape these poems, including Leona Gom, Bert Almon, Rhona McAdam and members of writing groups past and present. My deepest gratitude is to Mike Bartholomew-Biggs, for everything and honest criticism too.

My thanks to Elton Bash for permission to use the cover image by his wife, Elaine Kowalsky.

First published in Great Britain in 2006 by Flambard Press
Stable Cottage, East Fourstones, Hexham NE47 5DX
www.flambardpress.co.uk

Typeset by BookType
Cover Design by Gainford Design Associates
Front cover image: 'Beginning Memory II' by Elaine Kowalsky,
reproduced by kind permission
Printed in Great Britain by Cromwell Press, Trowbridge, Wiltshire

A CIP catalogue record for this book is available from the British Library.
ISBN-13: 978-1873226-86-5
ISBN-10: 1-873226-86-1

Copyright © Nancy Mattson 2006
All rights reserved.
Nancy Mattson has exerted her moral rights in accordance
with the Copyright, Designs and Patents Act of 1988.

Flambard Press wishes to thank Arts Council England for its financial support.

Flambard Press is a member of Inpress, and of Independent Northern Publishers.

CONTENTS

Chair of Truth	7
At the Border	9
Writing with Mercury	10
Wrong Toolkit	12
Risk Analysis	13
Chesterfield of Doom	15
Maze	16
Maps	17
Bitternness	18
Roses	19
Brownie Lore	20
Father Knows Best	22
Ubi Sunt Rotae?	24
Work of Equal Value	25
Doll	26
Canalside, March	27
Ceremony of Eels	29
Ice Fishing	30
Winters of Authenticity	31
Song for Canadian Dads	32
A Woman's Name	33
Old Baby Tales	35
Kimonos	38
Colombina at the Half Moon	40
Fourteen Women	42
Her Other Language	46
Third Generation Lost Language Blues	47
Four Translations and Riddles	48
Written in the Name of Rose	50
Of Weaning and Desire	52
When in Finland	54

Crossing the Floor	55
Stones of New Finland	56
Inheritance	57
Canadian War Memorial, London	58
Northern Way	59
Sod Hut	60
Grouseness	61
AWOL	62
Clock of Compromise	63
Swimming in Croydon	64
Meeting Karl	65
Footferry, Richmond	67
A Fine Romance	68
Miracle on Upper Street	69
Totem Pole Raising, Bushy Park	71
Rogues' Gallery	73
Farewell to Fag-ash Lil	74
Blackberries, Lumb Bank	75
Famous Blue Moleskins	76
Second Hat	77
'Tosi' is a Word for Truth	79

CHAIR OF TRUTH

The cushion on the chair of truth
is covered with yellow cotton
at first glance. Look again:
rows of navy lozenges
with red knots on a field of turmeric.
No birds or animals rampant or couchant
except the ones that clutch our shoulders
or those that lie uneasy
in our laps, almost tame.

Through gauze and distance
we tell the outlines of a story,
highlight the sunny bits.

A diplomat's daughter sat there once,
her tongue thick with tales of figs and honey,
tennis and croquet. Settling further in,
fingering an arm where the white had worn
down through the green to dead umber,
she told of childhood loneliness
in Persian corners and Dutch corridors,
how she hated chandeliers and cigars.

Yet she joined the Foreign Office herself.
She had a gift for languages,
a tolerance for solitude,
practice in discretion,
a taste for intrigue.
Born to it.

She floated through Germany and Burma
without a wrinkle, flourished in Washington.
Any friends she made she left.
Always the paramour, never the wife.

She said the quetzal
caught her by surprise:
the trade minister in Costa Rica
took her to the high-cloud forest
where she heard its two smooth notes
rising and falling in the mist.

Only once did the air clear
and the quetzal broke into view,
resplendent,
its emerald tail ribbons
sweeping the sky in iridescent swirls.
It screeched and was gone.

Her tears dried
on the chair of truth
leaving no damage.
She never returned my calls.

AT THE BORDER

In the line marked nothing
to declare I stood alone
and declared my solitude.
>No duty to pay on that, Madame.
>The officer was bored, demanded more.

Then I declare losses.
Of love, work, air,
self, light, memory –
>Madame, this list is too long.
>Three is the limit.

Love, then, first.
>That is better, my dear.
>You must pay in tears.

Second, a self that is whole.
>The line for damaged goods
>is through the yellow gate.

Memory and knowledge
count as three, agreed?
>Tariffs on intellect have yet to be decided.
>Wait in the room with the black door.
>It has safety glass and one-way mirrors.
>Tea will be provided,
>soup and bread twice a day,
>pen, ink and paper.
>
>We will be watching.

WRITING WITH MERCURY

Eyes upon me, though I cannot see
them or my own,
the mirror black
on the wrong side.

I have been called by so many
names I do not know
which to inscribe
at the top of the sheet.

Dip the pen into open ink –
no, it's a thumb-bowl of mercury,
bureaucracy's joke,
movable blob of a mirror.

I remember childhood warnings:
don't keep looking at it or your face will melt,
don't breathe it or you'll lose your hair,
don't touch it or your fingerprints will fade.

Pressed between thumb and forefinger
mercury skims across the page:
silverfish escaping from a torch,
twenty-six seductive drops of toxin.

Write with mercury?
May as well try to round up
minnows in a paper sieve
to make a wall-eyed pike.

Maybe I could use this pen as a needle,
thread quicksilver into a necklace;
maybe I could furl this paper to a point,
pour blood and silver in a glass tube.

Mercury freezes at minus forty,
where Celsius and Fahrenheit meet.
All I need is Canada in winter
and ice can be my medium, my weapon.

All I have is London in gray rain
that never freezes hard enough to matter.

WRONG TOOLKIT

The trick is to find the right tool
for the job, don't try to pound
an inchnail into steelhard plaster
with an improvised hammer – chisel handle,
stapler, shoe heel, stone: all you'll get
is a bent nail, a sore thumb and a scarred wall
where you visualised a picture.

All the tools you brought are useless here:
an accent that sounds Yank in the middle
of the Gulf War in a Labour neighbourhood;
ears so used to prairie vowels and chinook rhythms
that phrases filled with glottal stops
or plum-pit vowels are equally incomprehensible;
a belief in one true lightbulb, the kind that screws
into a socket, before the ironmonger tells you
most English bulbs have bayonet prongs.

Oh, they're friendly enough and call you luv,
and after they've mistaken you for American,
they say sarry, so sarry, and tell you about
their relatives near Toronto, do you know it?
The apology embarrasses you, but you scratch it
and find condescension toward the colonies,
and America-bashing so blatant you're shocked
into wielding an unfamiliar implement –
defence of a country more complex than
Coca-Cola, Hollywood and military swagger.

Finally you cringe at contact with strangers,
and ask your English friends to order your half of lager:
you know that if you ask the pub landlord,
you'll blurt out dollars or pennies when you pay,
and what you'll get is gin and sympathy.

RISK ANALYSIS

This is raw like meat left on the counter
for three days, brown blood in crusted
pools: I'm at the edge of the scab.

This is hard like green fruit, juiceless
oranges, gravel in the mouth, bananas solid
as table legs: I gnaw at their ankles.

This is rotten like overripe peppers and beans
forgotten in plastic bags, crude oil oozing
through breathing holes: I suck for air.

They told me risk was easy, fresh,
a click of the heels in mid-stride
and sometimes it is: jiving in the Barbican

to a hot band on Easter Sunday, a gift
in the interval between a Mozart mass
in St Paul's and a leg of English lamb.

They fêted me, toasted me, waved me off
on a cloud of kisses: 'Take my risk with you,
take it for me, have fun,' they said, and forgot.

They never said fun would go rotten:
fun is bright, fragrant cherry blossoms,
icing on the cake, forsythia flowing over

garden walls, profligate as buttered sun.
Hey presto, you're in Soho, sipping champagne
under a yellow canopy, a wench in full song,

a buccaneer's arm round your waist, his kisses
on your neck. What you didn't expect was the
alley, kneeling on cobblestones in raw wind,

your mouth inside his velvet trousers;
or waking alone in a rented bed, your nose
clotted, the smell of rats nesting under the tub.

CHESTERFIELD OF DOOM

Cut velvet. It invites us to lie
in luxury, seductive poses.
It promises wanton kisses, leaves
on our cheeks after too much wine
its ivy designs intertwined
with Jacobean cabbages,
the slobber of deep sleep.

Surviving all disasters
of cup, pocket or heart,
the chesterfield has no regrets,
absorbs the darkest spills and leaks,
they disappear into the deep purple
of its plush cushions, it swallows all
the lost coins that slip into its
crevices, welcomes the sodden
tissues dried to knots and balls,
you can only imagine the skeleton mice
on its underside in cruciform contortions.

Refreshment of bones after long work
is temporary: all who sit here
are destined to fray and mourn
just as all our ancestors
who traded labour for comfort
will never again kick off their shoes.

We are doomed to drag it from house to house,
this inherited upholstered beast
rigid as whalebone, tougher than horsehair,
it will last longer than mammoths in permafrost
smirking at moths and crusting scissors with rust.

MAZE

What I miss is gravel
crunching under foot or wheel,
wide sky above
the road straight into horizon.

I want to walk the crease
of a prairie book, lines of wheat
as even type, all one size
the word gold over and over.

London's a fused maze
of alphabets: wherever you walk,
each road, wherever it turns,
is utterly paved or cobbled crookedly.

A crazed typesetter has been at work
every night for centuries, his head
swirling with shadows thrown
on crumbling walls by candle-flame.

He has set every line diabolical
in a different font and size,
hot lead in higgledy-piggledy frames
and gutters overflowing with errata.

MAPS

I used to recognise
signs   stars   gestures

> The Flying Dutchman's pact with the devil
> doomed him forever to sail the oceans,
> but once a year, after midnight,
> he is allowed onshore.
> We met him in a restaurant
> overlooking Otter's Rock,
> he plied us with cognac.

I have forgotten several habits
perception   belief   intelligence

> We played pool in a sailors' bar,
> the roof leaked, a pail caught the drips.
> After you won the game
> (8-ball in a corner pocket)
> a woman with a shaved head
> challenged you for a tenner –
> you lost and bought her a beer.

I remember there were voices
    true meanings
I lived in several times at once
    coalescing

The maps I follow
do not show deserts or rain
treacherous mountain trails
places the car will stall
the brakes will fail
the beds we make love in
which I will cry in

BITTERNNESS

Memory is bittern:
one long vertical body
stretching into utter beak
hoping to pass as bulrush
and mostly it works:
the bird survives.

Walking the flat grass bank
of a River Lea sidechannel
I scan the reeds for bittern,
slide to the Nile of desire,
pick out the one straight pen
that shows against papyrus,
dip its nib into black water –
spring sloughs on rural routes
to Beaverhill, Alberta, where
I learned the ways of bittern,
listened for the low boom
from its narrow throat,
cavern of thunder, heard
or never heard – deluded?
Left home to follow a birdwatcher
who went to Africa so long ago
the country's name is – what
was his middle name, the story
about that missing flying boat?
Come now, bittern,
give me your drumbellow,
holler me even a lie.
You've slapped a memory on me,
now I want it to speak.

I finger the clamp on my rucksack,
let my longing slip to the reeds.
The bittern clicks into backdrop.

ROSES

A one-handed woman stands
in Canonbury Square, abandoned
on a pedestal. Rings of roses
circle her: whites, reds, yellows.

A snip of a child exclaims,
'This smells milk! . . . apple! . . . lemony!'
The woman says no names
for scents or colours, sees only

rows of hands clenched,
newborn-small, a frieze
of die-cut metal prints
in grays, the way a dog sees.

She is stone, without a chin
or nose. I occupy a wooden
bench, write to a man I'd given
wings, who breathed a virgin's

freshness into flesh
that youth had left. His eyes
were moments of day sky.
Cerulean, the ink dries fast,

envelope glue on the tongue.
It's a never-ending round
of flowers, paper, stone,
and making fist potatoes –

he will never read my letters.
The child is brushing petals
with her fingers to the sound
of husha, husha, we all fall down.

BROWNIE LORE

I never mastered the art of the lanyard,
the numbered and coded overing and undering
of hundreds of coloured plastic strips –
braided right, it wound up a smooth ideal
cord to hang around the neck, with a loop
for a safety whistle to scare off bears.
My lanyard always twisted,
my knitted scarf started out loose and oblong,
finished tight, triangular.
I cried Brownie tears at the sheet bend,
packer's knot, slippery hitch, reef knot,
pole hitch, sheep shank, timber hitch.
Brown Owl said these were useful knots
> *so my parcels would stay securely tied,*
> *my tent brailings tightly rolled,*
> *my pole bundles lashed;*
> *so my boat wouldn't drift away,*
> *my dog or donkey stray,*
> *my clothesline stay put,*
> *my flag remain flying.*

These were skills I had to know
to grow up jolly and hearty like Brown Owl,
wear a big brown uniform stretched
over a pillow-stuffed bosom,
sew badges up and down both sleeves,
use a whistle for the small brown girldogs
doing walkies in Indian file
around a giant toadstool.

We were pleasant little girls
in small brown dresses, ties and tams,
brown kneesocks and bloomers that barely
warmed our bums in Alberta winters.
> *Ladies and Brownies and Queens*
> *do not wear trousers, do not say bums.*

Brown Owl thought if I learned to make lanyards
I wouldn't take off my right mitten,
hold hands with Ricky at the Pleasantview rink
skating to Strauss by Guy Lombardo's orchestra;
if I learned to tie knots he wouldn't
walk me home through Mount Pleasant Cemetery,
kiss my tight lips under a frozen spruce,
my bare knees knocking.

If I grew up to be a Brown Owl
I could have horsey teeth and brown curly hair
like the Queen's on dollars and stamps,
and hunker down with the girls.
We could cross our legs like Indians
on the floor of Pleasantview Hall,
sing Iroquois chants from Ontario
with drums and syllables
around a paper campfire.

I could teach little prairie girls
a thousand miles from any ocean
to place their arms at clock angles,
send semaphore signals like sailors
across a hardwood sea to the distant shore
on the other side of Pleasantview Hall.
I could make them stand straight as yardsticks,
recite the Brownie oath, salute the Union Jack
and the woman in the diamond tiara
wearing a white silk ball gown
with a stuffed bosom
and a lanyard round her neck.

FATHER KNOWS BEST

called his TV daughters Princess and Kitten,
bought them velvet party dresses, rhinestone necklaces,
sat in his den reading the *Wall Street Journal*
but didn't mind when one of the girls burst in,
just had to talk about report cards, life,
values, all those deep things.

My father came home with plaster bits stuck hard
to his trousers, changed into clean khakis for supper.
When Mom cleared off the kitchen table
he spread out the *Edmonton Journal* to clean his gun
with bluing or shine his good shoes with vinegar and polish
the way he learned in the army. But he never talked
about the War or the Dirty Thirties, only ordinary things
like the difference between teals and mallards
laid out on the lawn in rows, how to dip them
in hot paraffin before you pluck them,
or how to tell perch from pickerel.
Some Friday nights he played poker with his wages.
Mom said that. She'd wait up reading Tennyson or Frost.
Some Saturdays he took us all to the horseraces:
he taught me to figure the odds, bet the quinella.

Father Knows Best came home on the 6:03,
made mortgage payments on a two-storey house
with a dining room, separate bedrooms for each girl
and Bud, the son. If they were in there sulking
he'd rap at the door, get them to open up about problems
with boyfriends or girlfriends or teachers
or not getting picked for the team.

My father kept moving us to low-rent houses
on vanishing prairie edges, finally right out to a farm
with 20,000 turkeys. I shared a bedroom
with my little brother, it had these dark pink kalsomine walls.
Sometimes he made me so mad I'd throw a hairbrush,
boy he'd scream, even if it didn't hit him.

Father Knows Best gave his grown-up Princess away
one day in June, little Kitten got to be bridesmaid,
he said they both looked so pretty, then he beamed
his warm krinkly eyes especially at the bride,
told her being nervous was natural
but each day would bring a surprise
and love would see them through the rough spots
but never turn the light out on an argument,
he went over and kissed Mother, just to show.

When I got married at 16, my father made sure
I didn't slip on the snow outside the church,
escorted me down the aisle proud and straight
like I was a proper woman holding onto his arm,
handed me over with just the two words –
he never thought he owned me anyway.
He danced me at the reception with a light touch,
a flourish, bowed when the waltz was over.

After my divorce I didn't want people
going on and on about time and wounds
or making examples of willow trees.
My father showed me how to change the oil,
got me to make out a will, join the motor association,
buy term insurance. When I got a chance
to go to Finland, he gave me a plane ticket,
drove me to the airport, carried my bags,
left me alone in security.

I saw his parting gift, a jacknife,
frozen on the X-ray of my handbag.

UBI SUNT ROTAE?

Where have they gone, the wheels of yesteryear,
those rubber tyres with wide white walls
dusted with clouds of perfumed talc
by tender hulks in T-shirts tight with pride?

Where have they gone, those hubcaps chromed
in chrome times four, their domes rubbed shinier than haloes?
Where are the shock absorbers that subdued
the gravel under Studebakers, Packards, Chevrolets?

No more double features at the drive-in
on the city's outskirts – where are the pairs
of dating couples in double-clutches
in front and back seats wide as chesterfields?

Gone are the movie reels, the giant screen
against a summer sunset, Ben-Hur in his chariot
racing James Dean in his hot rod
while Apaches and Comanches ambushed
wagon trains and stagecoaches,
their drivers dead with arrows in their backs,
as lady teachers clutched their collars,
collared preachers prayed and Annie Oakley
got her rifle out to help John Wayne
and a strip of a kid riding shotgun,
hooves and wheels a blur of dust,
sweat and heavy breathing.

Where are they now, those boys in ducktails,
girls in panty girdles? Last seen cruising
toward the suburbs without seatbelts,
trusting in bits of rubber and dumb luck.

WORK OF EQUAL VALUE

I told her the secrets of pie crust
with beaten egg and vinegar,
bun dough with cardamom.

> She never told me an hour's wage
> buys three bakery pies, a dozen buns and a cheesecake.

I taught her to shine mirrors
with ammonia and newspapers,
fill the house with wax and polish smells.

> She never taught me the tricks of nail varnish,
> the fragrances of Cartier and Chanel.

I told her to rinse her hair in lemon juice,
roll it in curlers filled with bristles,
sleep on the prickles, brush it out smooth.

> She warned me never to shave my legs
> or bleach my hair like Peggy Lee.

I taught her to iron pillowslips, French-corner
sheets, told her to lie in the bed she's made
with one husband until he dies.

> She never mentioned
> what else men do in bed.

She looks like a tart and lives in a sty
with streaky windows, a lumpy bed,
lives in sin with a man who drinks.

> She wants me to phone her every day,
> prays I'll marry again.

DOLL

This doll sits perfectly
    still
nameless and blank
mouth painted shut
    inarticulate
eyes painted open
    insomniac

She has a ribbon label
    stitched
on the back of her neck
black thread signature
    tattooed
by the woman who made her
    all she is
yellow hair to red
    fingernails

CANALSIDE, MARCH

In this mild unseason
between brown and green,
I fold the *Guardian* on the bench,
bluebells an uphill canopy at my back.

Two fishermen crouch
opposite me on the towpath.
Looking at one means not seeing
the other. Three points of a triangle,

we focus on our common
surface, water. Do they need fish
at all, or even the ripples that hook desire?
Or is it enough for them to watch reflections

of narrowboats, bare trees?
To watch until mortar re-melts
between liquid bricks, until drain holes
soften into singing mouths, until the towpath lip

contorts into grimaces, smiles?
The fishermen cast and wait.
Reel in, cast again.
Catch nothing

but ripples. Canal ripples
are not waterflow
but windbreath,
stagnant.

I refuse to remember griefs, identify
longings, ask how long I sit here.
Just hold on to emptiness,
unreason, unambition –

a new trigonometry.
To cry would be
a further grace.
I accept

dry ache.
Sorrow, not evasion.
Walk to the flat, listen
to Glenn Gould, pure north.

CEREMONY OF EELS

A winter break, a week without
the shallownine to dryfives for me;
all my friend from Lapland wants
is anything but snow, dark, trees.

We walk slow and local, inhale
the barny smells of cheeses,
gaze at pig snouts and tails
dried scarlet at the market, flinch

at eels writhing in the eel, pie
and mash shop window, each
constricted by a pale white hairy
hand, the body twitches

while a set of pale white hairy
fingers grips the knife, aims
quick at the point where bare
neck would be if bulbous head

were any part of eelness.
It is not. The eel is shorter
dead, but still a long thing,
now sliced along a thin line

from blooded top to tapered tail
by windowed hands abstracted
from the eelmonger, torso
disembodied by his task, matter, fact.

ICE FISHING

In pursuit of the silent pickerel
under a foot of snow, two of ice, a million sky,
the silent man, clad in layers
comes to the frozen lake

intent to force his world of hooks and air
into the fluid habitat of fish,
the dark liquidities sealed by ice
like paraffin on jelly.

He sharpens his spiral auger,
carves and perforates
a suddenly capitulating ice,
trepans the frozen skull.

Black water oozes up, fills
the vein between lake and air.
He drops a weighted line to plumb the depth,
ties a lure, sinks it, waits

hunched over the hole, hood against the light,
back to the wind, motionless for hours.
Random shadow-glimpses of the pickerel
jump-start his clotting heart.

WINTERS OF AUTHENTICITY

Universal as milkteeth,
the sliding gene is inherited
from the big white snowdaddy in the sky.
Even in London, where winter memories are black
from one round of children to the next,
the moment slopes are white, from Greenwich
to Parliament Hill to Primrose Mountain,
kids rummage antique sleds from attic closets,
or improvise with slices of cardboard, fertilizer bags.

Above the stranded *Cutty Sark*
we balance on icy walkways, talk
of historians, folksingers, art and authenticity;
lob a few theories and flights of wit
at syndromes and aesthetics.
Snow fills in our footnotes.
We anchor ourselves on a low stone wall,
sip Lagavulin from a flask – not the one true
single malt, but close. Sip. Reach the state
of higher logic. Sip. Ignore the cold.
> Remember how we ran our toboggans
> all the easy way up childhood hills,
> slid down whooping, free as coyote pups?

The Observatory looms
in twilight, a snowflake away
from the Prime Meridian, where
the West begins to rustle at 0°0'1".
It's a long way from the Rockies' Eastern Slopes,
where you will fly tomorrow,
sliding back through seven time zones,
114 longitudes.
Think I'll stay here for a spell,
try to make a snowball out of
next year I'll go home.

SONG FOR CANADIAN DADS

Once upon the Rockies' padded knees
we circled fires against the wolves,
sang road songs with refrains,
sang shanties, lullabies
and 'My old man's five hundred miles from home'

Once upon a folk song with throats
raspy from smoke and dew,
thirsty for tart red wine in a gallon jug,
we reminisced, told jokes
and harmonized on 'Baby done me wrongs'

Our fathers rode the rails and hitched
rides to logging camps and mines,
harbours, orchards, farms: anywhere
for work, anywhere for coal or gold,
wheat or lumber. 'Blackbird, bye bye'

Our fathers crossed oceans,
fought in wars they never started,
never spoke of courage.
Coming back, they cut a dash –
who wouldn't fall in love with them?

They married our moms and raised us in trailers,
cabins or prefabs in postwar suburbs.
We escaped to university
or jobs in boomtimes. Some dropped out.
'Within my heart's a hobo's broken song'

A WOMAN'S NAME

Long after I spat it out
for the last time,
that collection of confusible szyillapbulls
    phlegm in the throat
redundant vaouwaels
    tongue loose and thick among the teeth
spat it out, I say
spit, spat, spat
out that foreign surname
that roared its mastery for nineteen years
over my plain, forgettable name

    AND SHE SHALL BE MEEK
    AND SHE SHALL SPEAK ONLY WHEN SPOKEN TO
    AND SHE SHALL ANSWER TO HIS NAME
    AND SHE SHALL FORGET HERS
    (hiding in dusty wall-cracks)
    (nibbling on curls and slivers of wood)

Long after I've forgotten
the years of cramped survival,
the sudden release into a spacious room –
my own name, filled with breezes
and sunlight of childhood

Long after tentative forays into adult streets
now familiar territory,
awkward meetings with strangers
I now call friends

Long after I found it dangerous
even to think that
other name
I meet a man from that
other country, that
accent traps me, makes me
want to back away

Stories pour from his mouth
like the 300 kinds of beer in Belgium,
how his hometown doctor
cured a girl of anorexia by prescribing
a 40-proof cherry beer – one glass a day
loosened her resolve to starve,
gave her such a hunger she gained three pounds
the first day, just kept on chewing and swallowing
until she filled right out, round and shiny.

In a space between stories I venture that
other name in full Flemish accent,
wonder if he's ever heard it.
He writes its complication of letters
in exact easy order, tells me of generations
of pub-owners and storekeepers,
fishmongers and market gardeners
who set up their stalls by a river in Ghent
on a street that bears their name –
not a noble name, but respectable –
a long history of hardworking burghers
who know how to rub a copper coin
between thumb and forefinger,
turn it into a gold florin.

What to do with these snaps of accidental information?
Give them to my daughter. Maybe she'll go to Ghent,
walk on the street that bears her childhood name,
toss them in the river, see if they float.

OLD BABY TALES

Word baby

The mouth that sang me lullabies
taught me to touch her face with words:
    eye, nose, mouth   *silmä, nenä, suu*
    ear, throat, lower lip   *korva, kurkku, alahuuli*
These words got left behind in a Finnish trunk;
I never learned to say security, compassion.

Dream baby

The hand that leads me back through sleep
grabs my lower lip (*alahuuli*)
plucks a baby out with silver tongs,
the wound an empty cradle for an infant
thinner than a molar, shorter than a fang.
The tooth-child on my shoulder whispers
verses in my good ear (*hyvä korva*)
caresses the back of my neck, traces
finger mazes on my cheek.

Diagnosis

Babies can't be born from lips
except in dreams or Latin. Theophilus,
the doctor, says this is a cyst:
the mouth has held back saliva,
folded mucous into cheeselip
curled and hardened to a lump.

Surgery

Forty-five minutes of nothingness:
time into zero won't go.

Recovery

Theo smiles around his mask: 'It's gone, welcome back.'
The Irish nurse clucks and pats, tucks me into goose down:
'Sure you'll be missing your family, love.'
And suddenly I'm eye-deep in memories,
tell her what's been welling thirty years.

Tooth woman

The old wives got it partly right: you do forget
the pain, but not its metal cradle.
Now I set it moving, whistle through cold teeth.

Girl baby

Babies should not be born in corridors,
but a teenage girl in labour can endure,
in 1964, whatever uniforms dictate:
a different set of rubber fingers
up her public rectum every quarter-hour,
measuring dilation. Numbers announced
in loud centimetres to every passer-by.
Let the patient hide behind eyelids.
When she reaches 8, she gets a labour room.
Awkward as a calf, a student nurse
slips in – they were schoolchums once,
but in this place no one tells you how.
The girl asks the girl to hold her hand.
Contraction is one word they know,
when a strong one comes they forget
to breathe, all they can do is grip.

Wheel her into delivery, it's time:
lights, action, doctor, stirrups, noise.
Pain, colours, something something pain
something music, yes, and someone prayed –
light was voice was God was saying
let them both survive. A girl baby,
all dark hair, settled on my chest.
For seven days a further blur of fevers,
fluids, stoppages, indignities;
one nurse had a beak and claws.
But the doctor was attentive,
the Grey Nuns gentle and French.
   Hail Mary, full of grace, bonjour.

After words

The Irish nurse touches my cheek
in this private hospital, Harley Street.
'How's your daughter now, love?'
'Strong, beautiful, nurse, Canada, far.'
In a week or so the stitches
will dissolve in my lip (*alahuuli*)

KIMONOS

Mine is the mother's:

White cranes with red crowns
fly neckward toward a yoke
of layered triangular patches:
shooting stars in silver galaxies.
The blues of the cotton skies
for old cranes and new stars
match, the remnants picked
by a friend with a quilter's eye.
She loaned me needles and travel
scissors to patch the worn shoulders
and neck of my kimono. I've wrapped
its cranes around me seven years.
Who can count the threads in waves
of clouds, diagonal flocks of cranes?

Yours is the daughter's:

Sewn in Japan, sold in Manhattan,
wrapped in London, mailed to Canada –
your kimono's new but it has travelled
three continents to find you. I picture you
wearing it now, tall in black and gold,
its patterns on fans that trim the air as you walk
in scenes of nature, dreams of taming it:
    concentric arcs of waves;
        hexagons that frame blossoms
            of lotus, cherry, chrysanthemum;
                maple leaves on terraces and roofs;
                    bridges that curve from rivers to skies;
              boats in reeds whose tips end and end
              and never end in interweaving circles;
            singular doves that float among the fans
on random individual threads of wind.

Years from now, when your kimono's
wearing thin, summon me and I'll come
with needles and scissors; we'll choose
new fabric for patches to make it last.
Who can count the miles between us?

COLOMBINA AT THE HALF MOON

The moon guttered through the churchyard trees
when we emerged from the reading. Freezing.
Books tucked in bags, we dived into the Half Moon,

Rosy, Jenny and I taking Blake for a Guinness,
Heaney for a chat, Beckett for a date,
a bit of a long overdue catch-up in the pub.

We triple-clicked our drinks and a woman appeared
from the far side, white hair a hive
of bleached silk, face a floured pumpkin,

trousers and blouse loose on her boniness.
She swayed and doubled over, oh the pain in her ribs,
wobbled at a chair, sat herself down thank you at our table.

Levelled a half-eyed gaze at each of us in turn,
our faces a three-way mirror
of what she wanted, what she used to be

before she met the ferret, who put her in a sack
and beat her till her ribs cracked,
her face swelled bigger than a puffball.

Her name was Colombina and she fancied herself a seer,
offered to read our fortunes in the foam of a fresh beer.
Our eyes agreed to attend. She got most things wrong.

Yes, Rosy's a teacher but not a politician or a mother.
No, not Colombina's mother.
I suffered no loss two years ago.

Jenny's not involved with a man
with a four-letter name, such as Terry.
We mummed our faces not to laugh.

Addled by booze and singing the blues
Colombina struggled to remember
how to be with women, reached into her handbag

for a tissue, sorry for taking up our time,
did we really want to hear her story.
Her fingernails were perfect. Red.

An Italian from Clerkenwell, she'd longed
for the stage but never made the West End,
only Collins Music Hall. Always wanted

to play Isabella, who makes the men's tongues
thick, but she got stuck as Pierrot,
the clown so trite her lament became a mime.

Would have settled for her namesake, Colombina,
the serving wench who outwits all the men. Instead became
the butt of jokes, a Judy-bag for Punch's glove.

She was proud of her red shoes, pointed as lizards' tails.
They were her daughter's. No, her daughter's gone
and won't return her calls. But where is Rosy's daughter?

We scooped up our books, tied our throats with scarves.
She fluttered and cooed, would we be safe, said I'll be fine
myself thank you the weasel's taking me home.

FOURTEEN WOMEN

In memory of the fourteen women engineering students murdered on December 6, 1989, at l'École Polytechnique de Montréal.

1
Can't stop thinking about them
their names, their faces
    Nathalie Croteau
    Anne-Marie Lemay

2
Can't stop thinking about them
blood seeping and flowing
a leaking aneurysm.
Try making supper, liver:
flour can't absorb the blood.
Try chicken, there it is
oozing from the joints.
Try vegetables, can't bear
peeling skins, cutting off
heads and stems, snapping
spines, removing inner seeds.
Their skin, their hair,
their bodies wrapped in satin,
wood, frozen earth
    Sonia Pelletier
    Annie St.-Arneault

3
Try blanking them out with music,
try opera, Pavarotti singing
Ave Maria at Notre Dame in Montréal –
maybe some of them had been there
with their families, lovers, husbands,
had walked back to the Métro through the snow
arm in arm, full of music, glad to be alive
    Barbara Daigneault
    Maryse Laganière

4
Fifteen years on, in a London flat,
I still think about them in that classroom.
The details are lodged in every Canadian brain
but forgotten by the rest of the world:
how the man I will never name
ordered the men to leave,
rounded up the women,
called them a bunch of feminists,
how dare they study engineering.
I hear their pleas, whispered, desperate
arguments   denials   disbelief
panic   screams   silence

They still come to me at night,
disturbing the easy muddle of a dream –
say a dinner party, seaside cottage,
Chaucer toasting Margaret Atwood,
my mother playing mandolin –
they enter single file, stand behind each chair.
Everyone stops talking
    Geneviève Bergeron
    Annie Turcotte

5
Talk, that's it, get it back in the open
as we did when it first happened –
how we collected every detail
from newspapers, radio, TV;
how we listened and talked out
anger, guilt, confusion,
how we went to memorial services,
Canadian wind freezing our tears.
And the men didn't stop us, no
they joined us, that first week.
Later they got annoyed,
angry, wouldn't be implicated,
denied a connection between him and them,
his act and other men's attacks on women.

But we couldn't isolate him,
build a fence of logic
or madness around him
    Maud Haviernick
    Maryse Leclair

6

What we stopped was our public words.
In private we met as we always did,
told our stories, but told them whole:

The gang rape at 13
in the long summer grass
behind the empty rink shack

The years of beatings
never mentioned before
when we met for coffee,
talking recipes, talking kids,
talking books, talking ideas,
talking everything
except the bruises

The small aggressions:
cigarette smoke blown in your face
by a man you thought was attractive,
interested – he just laughed

The medium assaults
not serious enough to call the police:
your arms locked behind your back
by one man, while another gripped
your face in the vice of his hands
shoved his tongue into your mouth
when you opened it to scream
    Hélène Colgan
    Anne-Marie Edward

7
We're not talking inevitable
human wounds, not talking ordinary
women's pain, we're talking random
triggers for hatred, curses,
anonymous violence
    Barbara Maria Klueznick
    Michèle Richard

8
It still spills out after all these years,
thousands of cycles of blood remind us
it is good to speak these women's names again,
write them for new eyes,
whisper, chant or shout them now:

    Nathalie
    Anne-Marie
    Sonia
    Annie

    Barbara
    Maryse
    Geneviève
    Annie

    Maud
    Maryse
    Hélène
    Anne-Marie

    Barbara Maria
    Michèle

HER OTHER LANGUAGE*

She has had to learn
a language that allows only
words she can say without
the thick skin lines outside
her teeth going anywhere
near each other

in this language the teeth
aching and dry, one cracked
stay a certain distance away

this is her language until
the swelling goes down
days at least

it was his hands that did this

all she can say are ice words
stone words
dust words
tongue-against-the-teeth words
dull sounds through the throat

liquids are all she can swallow
through a thick straw
that hurts when it touches

the slot in her jaw cannot shut
its corners cannot turn
towards her eyes

*a lipogram

THIRD GENERATION LOST LANGUAGE BLUES

Your blood flows
through my heart, limbs, gut,
    but stops
at my Canadian neck,
dammed at the throat.
Your blood is mine
    but not
your tongue, lips,
language of your birth.

I am guilty of collusion in the accident
of my unchosen birth in post-war Winnipeg,
condemned to a life of English sentences.
I have learned them well, their multiple
undertows pull me down
into swirling possibilities of poetry:
    swyrl
from Scottish through Norse
    possibilité
from French through Latin
    poesis
from Latin through Greek

I cannot deny the delight
of tongue, ear, mind,
the polyrhythmic shaping
of my Canadian heart
    but now
I am beginning to hear
the words that English never speaks:
    suomea suruksi
    language sorrow
    laulun kieli
    language song

FOUR TRANSLATIONS AND RIDDLES

1
kulta is darling, *kulta* is gold
Lapin Kulta, Lappish beer, beloved golden beer
ilta is evening but in the evening
is *illalla illalla*

I found it in Lake Petays
swam naked after *sauna*
after midnight, maidens together
we drank *Lapin Kulta* on the dock
darling Lappish gold
sang vespers in twilight July
illalla illalla

2
peitellä, cover
jäällä is ice
pimeä, darkness
peitellä jäällä
cover of ice
jääpimeä peite
ice-dark cover

I dropped it in Lake Vesijärvi
rowed beyond the reeds
where Aino resisted the hoary charms
of Väinämöinen, wizard of song
(born old when the world began)
released herself down to the dreamfish
She holds it for me until winter
when sun is only a memory
encased in darkened ice
peitellä jäällä pimeällä

3
verinen is bloody
siipi is wing, *siipi* is blade
verinen siipi
bloody wing, bloody blade
kotka is eagle
kotkan siipi
eagle's wing, eagle's blade
puukko is dagger
puukon siipi
dagger's blade, dagger's wing

I found it in Helsinki airport
when the plane, metallic raptor
flew off with me inside its belly
I hid it under my skirt
beside a *puukko* in a leather sheath
Kauhava knife with a blood-groove
verinen siipi, verinen siipi
kotkan siipi, puukon siipi

4
kulta is darling, *kulta* is gold
kultainen, golden or *kultainen*, loved
koru is jewellery, *koru* is ornament
kultainen koru
golden jewel, darling ornament
kotelo, case or *kotelo*, pouch or *kotelo*, holster
kultainen kotelo
golden case, beloved holster

I left it in Copenhagen airport
on the last leg to Canada
shoved it inside a prostitute's
peacock leather purse
under her golden cigarette case
her gold-encrusted gun
kultainen koru
kultainen kotelo

WRITTEN IN THE NAME OF ROSE

i.m. Anna Mäntysaari Mattson, 1890–1983

If you lose her language you may as well burn
what's left of your grandma – her letters to *Liekki*,
Finnish for 'flame'. That weekly paper

came by mail, rolled up tight from Ontario,
its title set in red, all caps, and every letter
painted with fire that couldn't be banned

in Canada, immigrant heaven. Was she a red,
my grandma Anna? A farm wife in the whitest
clump of church Finns in Saskatchewan?

She had no politics that I could hear
with childish English ears, but oh she could hold
a kitchenful of visitors with stories

longer than the rugs she wove from old clothes
in eloquent symmetrics, wide stripes
in colours to match desire with design.

Her voice had the flex and cadence
of an actor's, but her handwriting,
self-taught, was tense and ink-blotched.

Her letters, never two the same shape or size,
struggled across the page like loosened threads
caught on burrs in underbrush.

Surely her thoughts were not so ragged:
decades of *Liekki* editors were keen
to decipher her scripts, print them in columns.

But why did she use a pseudonym?
'*Nimini on Ruusa*,' she claimed:
'My name is Rose and I can say anything.'

Whatever she wrote, it's all lost to me,
my eyes and ears clogged by the ashes
of Finnish, the only language she really knew.

Boxes of unsorted *Liekki* files
are stacked in the Archives in Ottawa,
her manuscripts among them, I assume.

Back issues on microfilm have numbers
but no index. Chronology's as useless
as English for finding my grandma's words.

Anna kept her articles, signed Ruusa,
tied in twine. They were burned by my aunts,
possibly in the name of tidiness.

OF WEANING AND DESIRE

Milk is the matrix of this culture.
I keep it alive in a hand-thrown cup
painted with a woman's face,
her hair an uncontrolled radiance.

> She was the woman who squeezed from her breast
> drops of her last milk
> before her last child was weaned,
> stirred them into a bowl of fresh cow's milk,
> let it sit all night beside the stove
> humming and warming to a lyric thickness.

> Bowl   cup   breast   song
> a spoon at a time the child is nourished
> by the bowl of cultured milk,
> she calls it *viili*,
> accepts its continual fullness
> as the infant accepts its mother's breast.

> The child grows to womanhood.
> On her marriage morning
> her mother unplaits and brushes her hair,
> blesses her with three gifts:
> a wedding rug in colours of spring,
> a hand-thrown bowl glazed in sky,
> a square of cheesecloth
> dipped in *viili*, dried in the sun.

> Take these with you, my daughter.
> The rug will warm your bed,
> give you children.
> The bowl is for milk,
> soak the cheesecloth in it
> and the *viili* will be reborn.

I am the one who must keep this alive –
it has been carried through centuries across borders,
even now the women conspire and hide
the dried cheesecloth in envelopes
undetectable by airport X-rays.

My breasts are dry, my children grown.
I live without custom, eat what I need,
cut my hair short. I keep this alive
not for my daughter, who does not know its taste,
but for my mother, for all the Marias,
their ancient desire confined in a cup.

WHEN IN FINLAND

In Kaustinen, first hour of midsummer,
last light blending into new light
at half before one   *puoli yksi*
I blinked and missed the night.

Dancers on an outdoor platform
moved in unison to a single accordion,
wildflowers fell from their hair.
I watched from the edge,
remembered the word for heart
and its first ending   *sydän, sydämen*

Two women emerged
from the willow-rhythms,
a man claimed one, the other claimed me.
I thought of a little bird   *pieni lintu*
She met my eyes on a held note,
raised me to the platform,
offered me the lead.

My right hand put itself
round the wrong side of her waist.
I had never danced with a woman
under the midnight sun –
my feet were blind,
arms unjointed, hands evasive
in a crooked-awkward *jenka*.

As we moved into a long-familiar waltz
light and forest took each other's measure
eye to eye   *silmästä silmän*
the forest took a bow
and every birch and pine
stepped forward into place.

CROSSING THE FLOOR

I have sat on benches in country halls,
tapping my Lutheran sandals toward
the man who reinvented the waltz,
only to have a much-married neighbour
beer-barrel stumble against me.
I have made do with mechanical turns
to the chorded boredom of *Lara's Theme*,
responded politely to tractor talk,
refused invitations for a nip in the car.
The custom of the dance, *tanssitapa*,
stays locked in Canadian immigrant time.

Here in Helsinki, old rules don't hold:
once a week the women ask. The men
are obliged to accept. At the first table
identical triplets in tight collars hold
their joined breath as I cross the floor.
The dry porridge of pre-feminist terror
fills my mouth: choosing one means
disappointing two. It's a cruel game,
bad on the hoping side, worse on the asking.

The night matures, I learn the cues,
check out hips, chalk up fearless glides.
Swaggering youths, gorgeous behind
their drinks, nervous on the floor,
are not the ones for me. I want
(a little victory, those words)
the ones with clear eyes, subtle moves:
the tango men, the debonairs of jive.

STONES OF NEW FINLAND

I am descended from common stones,
played as a child on their dumb round
shapes along the edges of fields
in New Finland, Saskatchewan.
Mounds of stones: my mountains,
my scatterdown castles with secret doors.

These were not the stones Frost used
for mending gaps in wisdom;
not the elegiac sighs of Wordsworth;
not the hearts and burdens
of wanting Brontë heroines.
I've traced their lines in England
and New England. There they were:
solid, shaped, magnificent.

The Saskatchewan ancestors
sit and squint, unshapely,
stones that say to me:
words are only words.
You cannot make us into anything
but what we are, or lug us
into houses built of useless paper.
We will not reveal our stories
and we will ignore yours.

INHERITANCE

On my fortieth birthday a pale man
in a silk suit delivers the deed
to a plot with straight hedges,
topiary trees, grass clipped
to the edges of a bronze plaque
inscribed with my name, birthdate –

I will not accept this –   gift?
    I want my bones   in a wilder
  place with shifting   borders
      where even bronze dis-
    integrates   to what it's made of –
copper, ash & tin   weeds/choke/out/grass
    fieldstones   litter the   land-
        scape   (annual offspring of glaciers)

The large stones are rage
the small ones anger
I have learned these words myself
not from my parents
    (whose calmness buried rage)
    (whose dignity smothered anger)
but from an ancient forebear
who deposited pebbles
in a pod below my heart
they grew one by one
climbed my gullet
filled my mouth

I have rolled them around on my tongue
spoken their forbidden syllables
strange at first as a foreign language
now I hurl them at the back of the silk suit
retreating down my garden path

CANADIAN WAR MEMORIAL, LONDON

Green Park has banned frivolity.
No ponds or flowers interrupt the lawns.
Plane trees stand in military rows.
A veteran strides alone, halts,
marks time before a brand-new monument
to Canada's soldiers killed in Britain's wars.

Glory is not on offer. The sculptor believed
in the grace of geometry. Sloping in parallel
from the veteran's chest to my ankles
are two granite slabs – a pair of continents
split by a corridor the width of hips.
We stare across generations, our mouths open
like caught trout. The medals hooked on his coat
glint like the spinners used for northern pike.

This is not a man I would approach
to say my father signed up in Regina,
joined the pushes north through Italy,
survived the killings he committed
with rifle, bayonet, bare hands;
the gambling and drinking to forget
(what I only know from uncles' whispers).

No rain, but the sculpture is wet.
Fresh plane leaves are sliding down a skin of
>water
>sky
>granite
>mirror

the leaves meeting their carved doubles,
brass incisions in the polished stones.

NORTHERN WAY

It's fine for some to say do not go gentle,
that a roar is more impressive than the quiet
options of a man who always measured words,
preferring wilderness to barstools, drunken chat.

Dad doesn't garden anymore: last spring
he sowed tomatoes but what came up
had fat green leaves, white blossoms –
eventual potatoes for his evening soup.

At fifty-three he traded in his guns
for clubs, the rituals of golf could satisfy
his need for reaching targets just as well,
get him out in the open, stretch his limbs.

Eighteen holes was an easy morning,
his handicap was low, his driving straight.
Now flags keep disappearing and he loses
count of strokes and saskatoons are ripe.

He picks a few to eat. When cranberries appear,
he sweeps the bushes with a putter,
jams his pockets full of dirt and fruit.
The stains are chokecherries, indelible.

Hugs are just as bad as confrontation –
Mom gives neither. He shrugs and wonders.

His is the northern way, where twilight fades
to morning without ever passing night.

SOD HUT

Last night my father phoned
from the wrong zone
    Saskatchewan mean time
    dementia standard
from his wire-crossed line
    moonlight saving time
    Finnish meridian
to tell me my brother loves me

'*Kuinka niin?*' I said to him
in baby Finn: 'How so?'
My brother only calls when news is bad
    Dad's on his death bed or Uncle Ed
    our mother's gone and taken a stroke
never just a trans-Atlantic chat

But if I can't trust
a man born in a sod hut
his immigrant father built
from blocks of turf
cut from native grassland
never measured never owned
until homesteaders claimed it
corner by corner
            who can I believe?

Earth walls absorbed
my father's first cry
    unmusical and raw
his mother gave birth on a straw tick
    unforgiving as darning needles

My father never theorized
or lied: I need his truth and call
my brother's answering machine

GROUSENESS

Memory is grouse wing:
the moment of extended thrill
when the body walks, all ear and eye,
through an autumn poplar wood,
the heart a waiting trigger
pulled into quick-fast-now
by the whir of grouse throat puffed right up,
the whip-whup-wupwupwup
of stuttered wings, demented feather engine.

Eager for the start of hunting season,
my father took me birdspotting
every year and every year
the routes were all the same to me.
To him each tree was marked, each field,
each prairie slough imprinted on his memory.
If sometimes, bored, I whined
he'd mutter 'Quitchergrousin'.

Here on an empty cricket ground
in Hook Heath, Surrey, a boy flings
his balsawood airplane into my reverie,
whooup-wup-wup-wup it goes,
hand-wound elastic band
driving the propeller
until it winds down
single-feather slow,
nosedives
into a softball diamond
at Lucky Lake, Saskatchewan,
one prairie gopher as witness.

My father's memory now:
grouse escaping, gone.

AWOL

He's back in barracks now.
This time it's permanent:
they snap his wrist
into an electronic handcuff.
If he breaks the doorway
radar beam, alarms go off
and wardens apprehend him
with a light touch, there now,
march back, three four.

Dignity walks slowly is the message
in a fortune cookie: not the usual
kind of loot the Easter bunny leaves,
but it's in the bag of goodies on his bed.
'I must be very dignified,' he says,
checks his watch. It has no hands.

CLOCK OF COMPROMISE

Like the gosling to Lorenz
mistaking the doctor's trousers
for maternal feathers,
like the newborn simian clutching
its cloth-and-wire surrogate mum,
I was imprinted to a mechanical robin
fixed on a clock face: metallic bird,
her life constricted between the stretch
of an elastic worm and the snap of its escape.
My infant self was transfixed
by the ticking repetition of a two-second drama
with three characters: persistent mother,
immortal worm, hopeful chick (never fed).

I was nurtured to need the time,
even made love with a watch on.
My last one had no numbers,
just two slim knives for hands.
Losing it was panic.
Adrift in nauseous eternities
I got greedy and sick for exactness,
addicted to public ticks and tocks,
church bells, furtive peeks
up other people's sleeves.

Gradually I learned to swallow vagueness,
fly on a cloud of unnarrowing,
the worm of time no longer my god.
Now the eyes glaze over before
the end of the evening news,
the body wakes by rote
with or without the robin:
> the clock
> my lungs
> the heart
> my soft alarm

SWIMMING IN CROYDON

In the night heat of my city flat
I hunch at my desk, a dry toad
who began the day in water
floating under clouds and cedars,
a distant cousin close beside me,
lazy mermaids in her father's pool.

We were both unclothed. The scarred back
that she never exposes to others
but sometimes mentions with pain
was suspended by water that kept her secret.

Her breasts and belly,
and the black happy triangle
where her legs part and begin,
bobbed and winked at the branches.

We swam as we were born,
in amniotic floating we returned
to the soft enduring arms
of Our Lady of the Oceans.

Our watery amnesia swept away
the men who no longer embrace us.
But earth and ink are cruel, the city night.
I blink against the chlorine in my eyes.

MEETING KARL

'History exists only for the need for consuming theoretical nourishment.' Karl Marx, *Die Heilige Familie*, 1845

Karl Marx eats the corn flakes of history
in my basement flat, with half-fat milk.
He's in London on holiday, moved to Alberta
after his reincarnation. His royalties
bought him a ranch in the foothills,
built him a log house down by the Little Bow.
The neighbours helped him raise his barn,
rounded up a band for the dance.
Karl learned the polka and schottische;
now he likes the old-time waltz best of all.

But he got to missing London, wanted to see
the old Round Reading Room one more time
before they moved all the books to St Pancras,
so he's back for a visit, incognito.

My gate creaks open and 'Allo, allo, allo,
wot 'ave we 'ere?' Comes a long pair
of Levis down the stairs, looks a coupla
duck-egg blues through my glass door,
a Clint Eastwood jaw behind my iron grille.
My keys are all thumbs, horn fish wriggling
on the ring. Cachuck goes the five-lever padlock
and over the doorstep step his hand-tooled boots.

A cowpuncher's life must suit him:
he's lost his scholar's paunch,
shaved off his beard to feel the wind against his face
when he rides out checking fences, surveying his herd.
His teeth are whiter than real against his tan.

Later, when we reminisced over wine
about our first meeting, lounging on the sofa,
his arm around my shoulder, we played
the 'I-was-more-nervous-than-you' game.
Neither of us won, but oh the jolly dialectic.

FOOTFERRY, RICHMOND

'I took Mick Jagger across
on the *Peace of Mind*,'
the ferryman bragged or lied,
pointing at Mick's pink
palace high above.

I fell in love with that skipper.
It was a brief affair –
     the Thames is narrow here,
     the crossing time short –
but intense. He dropped me

in nettles on the far bank,
the dead variety, *Lamium album:*
cream white flowers, stingless leaves.
Neverscratch. Neverbite.
Rare as true love.

A FINE ROMANCE

i.m. Gertrude Buckman, 1912–2001

Don't know a hawk from a handsaw,
fell in love with a falconer
in a field hard by Shakespeare's
mother's house, hey nonny,
oh the fine and bearded man:
one hand hid in a leather gauntlet,
the other stroked the falcon's
hooded head, smoothed its back
until the bird withheld her tremble,
melted to his will. She flew
straight for the bait he flung
on a string, raw meat spinning,
caught and flung again, hey nonny no,
glittering eye, talons grasping
leather strength of arm, wingbeats
swiping air, my air, the falconer's.

After dark I searched the grocer's
shelves for instant coffee – 'Hello,
don't I know you, would you share
my wine and partridges tonight?'
His hawking pouch was flat
against his leg, his glove was off,
and it had been a long time
since I'd tasted game.
                    There is a tide
in the affairs of hearts, which,
taken at the flood . . . de-dah, de-dum.
But not this time. I had a ticket for *Lear*
and Gertrude waited at the turnstiles.
Broke his heart, I know.
The arc of romance can be sharp
and cruel. His ungloved arm
bled with my rejection.

MIRACLE ON UPPER STREET

A face of mine, broken shell
in a heap of last year's straw,
invades the mirror, whose edges curl
and sneer like dried reptilian leather,
chemical scum on the beach.

Gabriel haloes my head with his hands,
oh there, the first stroke of my hair,
a choir in the distance is telling
good tidings, something about every valley.

Whence cometh thee, oh angel at my shoulder,
gentle tendrils round thy shining face,
thine eyes so blue? Florence. Of course:
the model for Fra Filippo Lippi.

A lesser angel from the Hackney side
of Paradise shampoos me –
it's his mum's birthday today, do I like London?
Massages my scalp, what's Canada like?
He can't imagine skies as wide as I describe.
> *Prairie winds blew round my innocence,*
> *my first love carved our names in a poplar tree.*

Gabriel's scissors are reluctant to begin,
but there is no transformation without sacrifice –
let the first cut be perfectly angled,
and the rest will be inevitable as waterfall,
with colours that arc through air, over rocks,
gather in a pool framed by columbines.

Fra Lippo, bring your palette,
push your easel through the crowds
of vain, ironic men and women
blind to all but bargains in antiques.

Observe the woman in Café Flo,
sipping orange juice alone,
radiant and quiet as her hair.
Only you can capture her
in tempera, transformed.

TOTEM POLE RAISING, BUSHY PARK

i.m. Elaine Kowalsky, 1948–2005

You scoffed at rope burn, your hands leather
from years of carving wood and cutting lino
for your prints: you could handle a press
better than a Wapping journeyman.

We dug in our heels and hauled in unison,
fashionable boots sinking like the hooves
of a pair of old cow moose into muskeg,
it was that wet, and cold as a Winnipeg spring –

July in London. Ropes in four directions.
We were in the western crew, breathing as one,
waiting to pull the slack until the drummer stopped
and the Nisga'a carver hollered 'Go!'

It was all new to us – the ritual singing,
the Squirrel Dance along the cedar pole.
Before the final hoist, everyone tossed
one treasure in the pit. You sacrificed

the art deco bangle in coral and jade
you found in a market stall,
I dropped a Virgin Mary medal
into the mix of earth, rain, gifts.

Drying off in the VIPs' whopper of a tent
you growled when the spirit of potlatch –
to give the best until nothing's left –
was broken by champagne inside

but only beer outside the chicken wire.
You trampled right across
with bottles of Bollinger for us
comrades, fellow celebrants,

planted your lips on the cheek
of a scarlet Mountie, poked the High
Commissioner's tum and grinned:
'What did they name you? Big Chief Grizzly B'ar?'

It was a day for givers and sayers of names.
The carver of 'Killerwhale-Eagle Pole',
Norman Tait, told his name in the Nisga'a tongue:
'Bear with no hair on one side, Enah-ahg-lagh.'

Elaine Gloria, daughter of Winnipeg,
baba's girl, Hackney woman,
I call you 'Artist with lightning hair,
bronze core, a soul that roars and roars.'

ROGUES' GALLERY

Loitering at wrought-iron gates
I inhale the traffic fumes and nicotine
more welcome to my lungs
than the trapped heat in a gallery stuffed
with dusty National Portraits.

I've left my American friend in Regency heaven
worshipping graven images of Jane Austen,
and said farewell to Tudor dames
with pearl-stiff torsoes, shaven pates,
emerald or garnet knuckledusters,
tight-lipped stares. No more can I bear
sighing maids whose boneless arms
wilt as they contemplate watery graves,
or those who inhale basil and pine
for cads who've kissed and spurned them.

Free from the double corsetry
of history and marriage, lucky me
who stands on Charing Cross,
an exile in loose trousers,
unafraid of the Irish vagabond
with breath that's been too long in a pub,
but charm enough to cadge a cigarette.

He cradles his hands around my lighter,
LOVE tattooed on his left knuckles,
HATE on his right. And yet
with gentilesse he honours me:
'You're an angel of mercy & an all-right babe.'

FAREWELL TO FAG-ASH LIL

When I didn't smoke
the last cigarette
from the last pack I smoked
I encrusted it with gold stars
silver foil diamonds
and spirals of seed pearls
cut from my wedding veil

I sprayed that last
oh yes alas unsmoked
cigarette with lacquer
placed it in a pine box
smaller than my hand
and lined with turquoise silk
frayed at the edges

Beside that jewelled icon
I tucked three earrings
     whose mates were lost
        at sea, in a dune, in a bar
a cutting of my hair
     when it was dyed red
and a feathered hook
     to snag the lower lip
     of an old trout

That box wasn't buried or burned
you can't destroy addiction
but you can wrap it up
consign it to a sealed case
in your own museum

BLACKBERRIES, LUMB BANK

'The drunkenness of things being various.' Louis MacNeice

Balancing on the garden wall, we spy
a suddenness of blackberries down the hill.
If they're ripe we'll gather them to garnish
cheesecakes for a crew of hungry bards.

You volunteer to recce the path and check
the berries' readiness, report their plump
cadenza of hellos: 'Taste me, choose me,
pick me, eat me, eat me first, tra la la!'

What is that brick-lined chamber in the slope
above the berry patch? Aha, the roof
reveals a porthole open to the sky.
Mystery-novel fans, we lean our heads

together: 'Elementary, my dear poet,'
you declaim. 'In horse-and-brougham days,
manure was shovelled down the chute.'
Our poems in many drafts are compost now.

We revel in our cleverness, imagine
aboriginal discoveries
of herbs to stew and dyes to paint the skin.
The sun unwraps our tongues, we think about

the clothes that could be flung, but aren't.
Our bowls are filling fast, we slow the pace.
We could eat every blackberry now, but don't.
The world is new; greed is not our style.

This is how legends start: woman, man,
perpetual fruit, desire, garden wall,
the drunkenness of berries being various –
even saskatoons are possible now.

FAMOUS BLUE MOLESKINS

after Leonard Cohen

It's four in the morning, the end of September.
I can't sleep, you're not here, my belly is painful.
London is muggy, the window is open.
My passport is useless, there's no rain, I miss you.

> *My father is losing the maps he has followed.*
> *Perhaps Canada misses me, the prairies are endless.*

And you came by with a map in your hand,
you said it had drawn you to me,
no matter how damaged I am.

The last time I saw you was yesterday morning,
you left in your car but you phoned in an hour.
I went to the office, I ached for your presence,
your photo beside me at work as an anchor.

> *My daughter has married a man from Alberta.*
> *I sent her a letter in a box with a key.*

What can I tell you, what can I offer you?
Nothing seems valid to say.
We went up for dinner, you wore your blue moleskins,
we spoke about angles with Robert and Linda.

> *Your daughter is worried you're losing your balance.*
> *She misses her mother, I'm glad that you loved her.*

And I came up on a train to the north,
you said you'd be waiting for me,
and you kept your word.

SECOND HAT

The last time I wore a hat
I was a Catholic. Improbable
helmet of pastel green polyester flowers.
A woman's head uncovered was dishonourable:
something to do with Corinth, Paul's correction rod,
centuries of bishops and popes in mitres,
those power hats of stiffened Gothic cloth.
Ordinary fellows clipped their headgear to pewhooks.
Some women pinned mantillas to their beehives.
Jackie, the model wife, stuck a pillbox
on the back of her lacquered hair,
or draped her whole head in black lace,
especially after JFK was killed.

After Vatican II and Vietnam
so much got blown away. Women prayed
with just hair, charismatics spoke in tongues,
played guitars. Latin faded.
Many got divorced, left a church
with space for the widowed, celibates and virgins
but none for the never- or no-longer-married
who didn't sleep alone.

Years pass and hats are so irrelevant.
Wind in your hair helps you think
you don't miss communion much:
there's nature, theatre, art, friends, careers.

This is the cue for happily ever secular
but sometimes grace appears. I skipped
down a second aisle without a hat or veil;
God seemed OK with that.

On or off, hats have lost their power
to confer propriety or shame.
God has more important things to do
than be a fashion guru, though she delights
in colour and form.
                    Now I'm whistling Wesley,
sewing silk azaleas and pheasant tails
to clouds of tulle on a plain white boughten hat,
primping it up as stepmother of the bride.

'TOSI' IS A WORD FOR TRUTH

In the Finnish language
a fact is a truth-thing, *tosiasia*
I want to say old words
with my truth-mouth, *tosisuu*
I want to roll wishes
on my truth-tongue, *tosikieli*

I want to eat wishberries
swallow the truthpips
wash out my mouth with breadsoap
quench my thirst with springdrops
Blessed are the waterpoor

I want to climb truth to the moon
on rope rungs braided
with reeds from my wishbed
Call it a ladder of need
Blessed are the spiritpoor

I want to avoid the mawkish cracks
the rags of mangled prayer
the truthslap that marks the cheek
with a hurtprint that never fades
Blessed are the touchpoor

I want to hang my wishcoat
my spun linen dress and velvet scarf
on truthnails pounded on the walls
of a bedroom with no wardrobe
Blessed are the homepoor

I want to cross the threshold
of my grandmother's kitchen
use wishherbs from truthloam
follow recipes in her birth tongue
Blessed are the wordpoor

I want to paint wingtruths
with coyotetail brushes
sketch longing with charcoal
from scorched pinelimbs
Blessed are the artpoor

I want to ride Hubble to the stars
and see if each lightpoint
is a hole punched in shot silk
by God's own truthpick
Blessed are the laughpoor

I want, I want: *haluan, haluan*
Haluan is my name